FEEL GOOD CLUB

FEEL GOOD CLUB

A GUIDE TO FEELING GOOD AND BEING OKAY WITH IT WHEN YOU'RE NOT

AIMIE AND KIERA LAWLOR-SKILLEN

WILLIAM COLLINS

William Collins
An imprint of HarperCollins*Publishers*
1 London Bridge Street
London SE1 9GF

WilliamCollinsBooks.com

HarperCollins*Publishers*
Macken House, 39/40 Mayor Street Upper,
Dublin1, D01 C9W8, Ireland

First published by William Collins in Great Britain in 2022

2

A catalogue record for this book is available from the British Library

ISBN 978-0-00-854652-6

This book has been written by the authors based on their own
experiences and knowledge, the advice in it should be used to complement,
and not replace, medical advice. If you are suffering from any mental
health issues always seek professional medical advice.

Printed and bound using 100% renewable electricity at CPI Group (UK) Ltd

MIX
Paper | Supporting
responsible forestry
FSC™ C007454

This book is produced from independently certified FSC™ paper
to ensure responsible forest management.

For more information visit: www.harpercollins.co.uk/green

To our parents,
without whose love, support and acceptance,
we wouldn't be on this journey.

HELL GOOD CLUB

FEEL GOOD CLUB

Contents

Note to reader

Dear Human,

Welcome to Feel Good Club: A Guide to Feeling Good and Being Okay With It When You're Not.

We're not claiming that this book will fix everything. In fact, we're actually not claiming it'll fix anything at all, but something brought you here and we're glad that it did.

We want you to know that however you're feeling right now is valid between these pages. This book is a safe space to feel your feelings, be inspired, laugh, cry, and remind yourself that although not every day will be a good day, you still have so many good days to look forward to.

This book is about reminding you that you are only human and humans have good days and bad days.

People forget to text back and they make mistakes but, most of all, at some point in life, everyone needs a little help along the way and we need to normalise talking about that.

If you follow us on Instagram, you'll be familiar with our reminders. We write and post them each day, based on how we're feeling. Sometimes it's things we need to hear ourselves, and at other times it's something we've learnt in the past.

This book will dive deeper into the meanings and experiences behind these posts, with the focus constantly on our general mental health.

What we really hope is that, in some way, our words will make you feel less alone with how you feel.

We don't have all the answers. We're a work in progress too because, guess what . . . nobody ever really has it all figured out.

Each chapter is dedicated to a particular area, or feeling, that we have struggled with ourselves, and each follows the same format to help you with easy navigation. There is a 'Menu' at the start showing

*the topics covered; 'Dear Human . . .' sections
addressing the reader directly about the problems
at hand; 'Feel Good Tips' offering practical
exercises to help you along the way; and finally,
some 'Takeaways', summarising the main points
of each chapter.*

*The book is designed to be kept with you in your
bag, or in your pocket, so you can flick through
to a relevant page or quote wherever you are,
whenever you need it.*

*Thank you for letting us be part of your journey
and thank you for being part of ours.*

Love,

Aimie and Kiera

About us

Wow! We're actually here, writing our own book, and you're here reading it.

If someone had told us seven years ago – when Kiera was recovering from an eating disorder, and trying desperately to start a business to keep herself busy while Aimie was at work – that we'd be here now writing this book and running this business, we'd have told them to p*ss off.

And if someone had told us that all we needed to do was to actually start believing in ourselves, we'd have probably told them to f*ck off instead.*

---

* We're being dramatic when we say, 'all we needed to do'. It actually takes a lot of hard work, ups and downs, risks, and showing up when you really don't feel like you can. But in order to do all that in the first place, you really need to believe that you can.

But that's what happened – as soon as we stopped worrying about what could go wrong, focused on what could go right, and believed that we'd figure it out along the way, things started to happen for us.

In under two years we'd secured investment to open our first Feel Good space (mid-pandemic, might we add!), launched our merchandise line, and now reach over 300,000 people every single day with our positive messages.

But contrary to what the world of social media tells us, things don't just happen overnight. Okay, maybe some things do . . . like the afternoon before we went into the second lockdown when we posted *5 Things you should hear as we go into the Second Lockdown* on our Instagram page, while making avocado toast in our coffee shop ourselves, because we couldn't afford any chefs. Then we received hundreds of messages and notifications, and saw that our Instagram page had grown by 100,000 followers in twenty-four hours! But the truth is that *most* things do not happen overnight.

When we reflect on Feel Good Club, we realise now that so much of our lives led to this moment:

the heartaches, the failed ideas, the Monday mornings stuck in traffic wondering whether we were actually cut out to do that for the next fifty years, and especially our own struggles with mental health . . . all these things played a part in us giving birth to this business.

The contribution of all those things, and because it's our baby, is why it's so personal to us. Those things are also the reason that starting Feel Good Club was never about creating the most financially successful business in the world, but about being the voice we needed to hear when we were struggling most.

●

We – Aimie and Kiera – are the wives behind Feel Good Club. We met at university in 2009, and were constantly doing something: starting businesses, putting on club nights, or organising (the best) house parties Stafford had ever seen. Aimie was the organiser and Kiera was the musician working towards a record deal that she later turned down, to prioritise her mental health.

Neither of us were at uni for very long before we realised that we definitely weren't there for the lectures. But looking back, we now understand that what we learnt there taught us so much about what we needed in our journey to starting Feel Good Club. Nope, it wasn't business – we didn't study anything like that – but the freedom to create and find ourselves, as well as the people we met, who later became good friends, all gave us the tools and passion we needed.

After a whirlwind first year together, we decided to take a break in our relationship. It was around this time that an eating disorder really started to take hold of Kiera. It spiralled out of control and the pounds began to drop off her. She'd always been the 'fixer' in our various ventures – the one who was always okay, the one people went to when they needed help. So, she felt she couldn't possibly be the one to ask for it. It's only now that we both realise how much support she would have had if only she'd allowed herself to open up.

A couple of years in, Kiera arrived home to her parents in Birmingham to find dinner on the table, so she used the same excuse she'd used a million times before: 'Don't worry. I had a McDonald's on the way home', then ran upstairs for a bath.

It was the days when, after a night out, people would upload loads of pictures to Facebook. But this time, as Kiera scrolled through the ones that had been posted, something clicked in her head and she finally saw what she actually looked like. Her hair had started to fall out and her bones were visible.

At the same time, Aimie sent her a message: *You look terrible. Are you okay?*

This was when Kiera's recovery started. She read thousands of articles, watched hundreds of documentaries, and started to learn more and more about her own mental health and how to improve it.

One of the biggest turning points was starting the earliest form of Feel Good Club, in 2014. Kiera was still struggling with on-and-off recovery and decided she needed something positive to focus her time and energy on, so she started the very first Feel Good Club Instagram page – an extremely cheesy version of what it is now. It actually did pretty well but, without any money to invest in it, she ended up getting a 'real job' as Head of Happiness for a social media agency, and Feel Good Club was put on hold. But we both always knew we'd come back to it.

After getting married in 2019, we did just that, and Feel Good Club was born again. Our first stumbling block was financials, as we had nothing to invest in the business, but knew that the original reason we'd wanted to start it was too important to ignore. Then just as we were about to give up, we got a mystery £500 refund from Airbnb (we promise to pay it back if it turns out to be a mistake!) and decided to buy a screen printer and teach ourselves how to use it, with the idea that wearing a piece of Feel Good Club merchandise would remind everyone of the things we stood for and talked about online – a reminder that good days were on the way.

We started the Instagram page with no expectations, just a goal to make one person feel better about themselves each day, and to be the voice that Kiera had needed to hear when she was struggling most. The things we discussed on Instagram – talking about mental health and feelings in general, and normalising the discussion – started to resonate with people. And even though we got off to a few faulty starts with our screen-printing skills, the clothing started to do well too.

Ultimately, what we wanted for Feel Good Club was a physical space. We'd dreamt of owning our own coffee house, bar, and events space for years, and it felt like the perfect way to take what we talked about online into the real world and provide a safe space for people to come to, no matter who they were or what they were feeling. A space to meet people, learn new things, and bring people together.

Even though we couldn't see a world in which this would be possible without winning the lottery, we kept talking about it. We put it on our vision board and wrote on our fridge: *Feel Good Club Coffee House, Northern Quarter, 2020.*

Every morning before getting ready to leave for a job she hated, Aimie read that sign out loud, determined we'd get there one day. It's funny to think now how much we believed we'd get there, even without any solid means of doing it.

One evening we sat in a bar after work and Aimie finally said she wasn't happy with her job or the life we were living: working 9 to 5, spending our weekends drinking and watching Netflix.

So, we made a plan: if, by the end of the year, we hadn't reached 10,000 Instagram followers – something we'd never been too concerned about, but which felt like a milestone – and if we weren't at least in talks about opening a coffee shop, then we'd pack up and go travelling. We shook on it, but nothing could have prepared us for what happened next.

We can't really remember when we hit 10,000 followers – as we said, followers have never been a metric of success for us, only a way of seeing how many people we could potentially help – but we certainly remember the day our dream of opening a physical space became a reality.

Kiera's role as Head of Happiness had turned into Global Director of Happiness and Culture. The role grew to developing and maintaining a great work culture with mental health at the forefront, and pretty soon she was doing that for the company's Manchester, London, Berlin, and New York offices. And from this, we gained one of the most beautiful friendships we could wish for.

Atul is the person to whom we owe so much of our journey. He's an incredibly talented interior designer and all-round bundle of joy. Kiera and he became really close after working together for more than five years. During Kiera's final year at work, before Feel Good Club, she and Atul took a trip to New York to design a new office. When they were there, she told him about our plans for Feel Good Club – the first time either of us had told anyone exactly what we wanted to do.

He turned to her and said, 'Well, let's make it happen.'

The following week he turned up at the office, after having told one of his clients about our dream. This client was interested in supporting us in making it happen, but wanted to see our business plan.

Exciting, right? Except we didn't have a business plan, and we'd never written one, just a vision board and, as we explained before, our goal for Feel Good Club had never been financial, so a business plan had never crossed our minds.

Kiera just said, 'Sure, we'll send a business plan over.' Then she went off and screamed down the phone at Aimie from the car park, and told her to start googling how to make a business plan.

Twenty-four hours later, it was ready and had been emailed to the person concerned.

Everything was guesswork: the maths, how many staff we'd need, what we'd sell, how we would learn to make coffee, what coffee machine we needed. That's when we met Howard, the person who made it all happen for us.

Howard started his property business in a similar position to us, with an idea and a dream to bring his passion to life. Like us, he also ran out of petrol on the way to his first meeting to secure financial investment for his business. He ended up running all the way to the meeting point, to make it on time and hasn't looked back since. Now that his business is going from strength to strength, he is in a position to help others follow their dream, just as he has done for us. He loved the idea of Feel Good Club so much, that our physical space now occupies the ground floor of one of the buildings his company manages. It's hard to believe that he agreed to lend two strangers, with absolutely zero experience, the money to open a 3,000 ft^2 coffee shop and bar, based on a business plan that actually said we'd make a loss in our first year (we didn't want to build our hopes up just in case!), and that talked more about how we'd make people feel than what we'd sell and how we'd make money.

But he did agree to lend us the money and that's how we knew he would be the perfect person to support us in our dream. The financials were never questioned – he saw our passion and believed in us, and so we got to work.

A couple of months later, a lot of our guesswork had been brought to life, and we opened the doors to our dream space, in our home city of

Manchester, two weeks before the second Covid lockdown. We hadn't been open long enough to claim furlough or any support grants, and we quickly realised that hospitality was far harder than knocking out a couple of coffees and toasties. However, working seven days a week as a takeaway outlet taught us pretty much everything we needed to know.

Once again, we began to focus on how we could support more people.

We covered our city with billboards displaying positive messages for anyone that was struggling, hoping to brighten up their daily lockdown walk.

We hosted a live, positive weekly news segment on Facebook with Manchester's Finest, a local media business that shared our ambition of spreading messages of hope and sharing good-news stories from the city.

And even though it was a tough year full of worry, big lows, and really high highs, we survived, and we owe all that to our team, the Atuls, the Howards, and everyone in our Acknowledgements and beyond, who kept believing in us and pushed us forward, as well as the more than 300,000 people who joined our Instagram journey and kept our business afloat.

But this book isn't about business – we'll save that for when we know a bit more about it.

1

When everything goes wrong

Dear Human,

We want you to know that things do, and will, go wrong. This isn't something we can escape or hide from, no matter how hard we try. No matter how much we overthink, or if do everything in our power to make every little thing perfect, there's absolutely no avoiding the fact that something will go wrong. Some days it might not. Some days it might be one tiny little thing that we can move past quite easily. But on others days these little things will feel catastrophic, like everything is falling apart and it'll never be right again.

But we are here to tell you that things will be okay, things will get better, and things will go right for you.

Just because things are going wrong it doesn't mean that you are wrong.

JUST BECAUSE THINGS ARE GOING WRONG IT DOESN'T MEAN THAT YOU ARE WRONG.

We've all been there. It feels like you can't catch a break. A series of really sh*tty situations make it feel and seem like everything is going wrong, like everything is falling apart.

Feeling like this is totally normal. It's not dramatic. It's not over the top. Everything is relative to you. And when we're faced with a number of difficult situations that have varying levels of impact, it's natural to feel like they're affecting your whole life.

But this is a reminder to stop, take a breath, and ask yourself calmly and seriously: Is *everything* going wrong? Are there areas of your life that remain good, consistent, and enjoyable?

If the answer is 'No', let's move forward. Let's see which of the things that have gone wrong are still within your control. Can you make them better?

●

We had to learn very quickly how to be okay with things going wrong, and we can tell you – practice doesn't always make perfect. There's not a special tool we can give you to make you okay with things going wrong. And there's not really anything we can tell you about how to handle each situation. You can only control what you can control and you will learn from everything else, even if it doesn't feel like it in the moment.

We can't even tell you the number of times we almost gave up on Feel Good Club, because everything felt terrible and left us questioning why we had been so naive to think we could do it.

For example, when we released our first line of merchandise, we thought we'd covered all the bases and done everything we could to avoid anything going wrong by setting up a pre-order. That way we could manage the number of orders coming in and get them out on time, right?

Wrong! We launched pre-orders twenty-four hours before the site went live and they started rolling in. Okay, the majority of them were from family and friends – maybe just our parents actually! – but as we got ourselves set up to start printing, our screen broke. Plus, we'd only got as far as learning on YouTube how to actually make T-shirts, but hadn't got to the bit about what happens if the equipment breaks down.

After a couple of hours of trying to fix it, trying to make new screens (each one takes eight hours), calling local suppliers (who wanted to charge us more to print than we were charging for the actual T-shirt), and Aimie crying at the top of the stairs saying this was all a stupid idea, *everything* had gone wrong!

The business was over.

We needed to de-activate the website, delete the Instagram page, and tell Mum she wasn't getting her T-shirt.

Instead, we did the only thing we knew we could do in order to calm down and process the situation – we had a cup of tea and reached out to a friend.

The following is going to be a common theme throughout this book and might be one of our biggest pieces of advice: when times get tough, you cannot go it alone.

WHEN TIMES GET TOUGH, YOU CANNOT GO IT ALONE.

Never be too proud to ask for help, even if you think you should have all the answers.

None of us have all the answers.

Without that crucial FaceTime with a friend in New York, who had experience in screen-printing and guided us step by step through how to burn a new screen, and highlighted that we were using far too much ink, we'd have been convinced that the whole business was going wrong, when in actual fact, it was a very small blip.

After this, every time we reached a milestone with the business, something would happen that would make us doubt the whole thing.

For example, on our first day of doing takeaways, the car ran out of petrol on the motorway, leaving Kiera to walk to open the shop, while Aimie hunted down some fuel.

On our official opening day, we realised that with our lack of experience, the kitchen was too small for the number of people we needed to fit into the space, and then the heat from the oven started melting the walls. And when we say melting, we mean *melting,* resulting in smoke everywhere.

Despite this, we still had to drag the team out of the back door as they didn't want to stop service.

Two weeks later, we went into lockdown, with no furlough or grants . . . the list goes on! But we'll save that for another book.

So, when it feels like everything is going wrong – without downplaying how *you* feel, because it's important that you allow yourself to experience all your feelings – take a deep breath, break it down, reach out to a friend, or take a moment to ask yourself: Is *everything* actually going wrong? Or is a series of crappy situations making you feel like it is?

NONE OF US HAVE ALL THE ANSWERS.

Dear Human,

Things are going to go wrong, but they are also going to go right for you.

Everything you've just read above could have easily convinced us that starting this business wasn't for us; that it'd be better to close it up before we took on any more commitment, and should just jump back into our lovely, cosy comfort zone.

Even worse than that, it could have made us terrified of doing anything. The experience could have made us too scared to move forward with new ideas, fearing that things would go wrong anyway, and that the stress of that would be far worse than staying where we were, ticking over.

But actually, what happened when all those things went wrong wasn't a life or business left in pieces, it was instead a steep learning curve.

THINGS CAN AND WILL GO WRONG, JUST LIKE THINGS CAN AND WILL GO RIGHT.

Time and time again we are asked whether we'd change anything about our bumpy start to the business, and our answer is always a firm 'No'. Out of each negative, came a positive:

- The car breaking down taught us that we can't get so caught up in day-to-day things that we forget to be adults and put fuel in the car.

- The kitchen issues taught us to adapt our menu into something far better than what we originally had.

- Not being eligible for furlough and support literally put our business in one of the worst possible positions that we're ever likely to be in, but we came out stronger because of it!

We learnt how to navigate all these issues, to communicate, and move forward.

TOO MUCH POSITIVITY IS TOXIC.

Even though Feel Good Club is a brand that promotes positivity, we are extremely mindful of the fact that too much positivity is toxic. Toxic positivity is the belief that, even when things are at their worst, we must put on a brave face and maintain a positive mindset. But ignoring the fact that things will go wrong is toxic. And ignoring the fact that, as humans, we'll make mistakes is also toxic.

It can be really hard to admit to yourself that things in life will go wrong. Realistically, lots of things go wrong. You will make mistakes. People will be mad at you. But guess what? That's not something that only happens to you. It happens to us all and, once we accept that, we can start to move forward without fear and focus on what could go *right*.

Because for everything that goes wrong, lots of things also go right. There will be times where absolutely everything slots into place.

We call our favourite days, when nothing extraordinary happens but nothing terrible happens either, 'Comfy Days'.

We have a nice time. We laugh with our friends without pangs of anxiety or worry. And we've made a mental note to appreciate those days a bit more.

Maybe you could try it too?

FEEL GOOD TIP

When everything feels like it's going wrong, it's hard to see a way out. So, don't keep it all in your head. Write down everything that's going on and try to identify *one* thing you can do to make things better. Small steps, deep breaths.

Identify one thing you can do to make things better. Small steps, deep breaths.

Dear Human,

We know how it feels to have thoughts whizzing around your mind so quickly that it feels impossible to pick one out. We know how it feels to try and keep it together, when internally you're trying to figure out how you're going to solve all your problems alone.

We're here to tell you that if you feel like you're the only one trying to figure it all out without any help, you're not. Most importantly, we're here to tell you that you don't have to try and do it alone.

Maybe you're like Kiera, who we call 'the fixer', as it's become part of her identity to be the problem-solver, to not let problems get to her (on the outside anyway), and to want to deal with everything alone.

Or maybe you're like Aimie, a chronic overthinker, who is able to express her feelings, but finds it hard to see a way out when things are overwhelming.

Either way, we want to remind you that you are only one person and, sometimes, we have to admit that we can't keep things to ourselves.

There is always a way out, but we can never see it while everything is whirling around in our minds. Admitting that we need help is not a weakness.

One of the best pieces of advice Kiera was given was from her Year 9 Head of Year. She was failing in Maths and Science (and any other subject that didn't spark creativity!) At this point she'd learnt how to record music and was spending the majority of her time doing that rather than her coursework, which was piling up.

ADMITTING THAT WE NEED HELP IS NOT A WEAKNESS.

In true fashion, she kept it all to herself, hoping it would just disappear, but during a parents' evening it all came out. Kiera told her Head of Year that she just didn't know where to start. So, the Head of Year sat her down and asked: 'Kiera, how do you eat an elephant?'

Kiera's instant cocky response was, 'I don't. I'm vegetarian!'

The Head of Year didn't acknowledge her stupid response, and instead told her: 'One bite at a time.'

Kiera pretended the advice had gone in one ear and out the other but now, fifteen years later, she still thinks about this advice every time things get overwhelming.

When things get too much, when it feels like you can't see a way out, think about that elephant, whether you're vegetarian, vegan, or anything else. We want you to think about how *you'd* eat it . . . metaphorically.

FEEL GOOD TIP

Get your notepad out and write down every single thing that's playing on your mind, from the smallest things to the big scary ones. It doesn't matter how long it takes you to write this list. It doesn't matter if it fills your whole pad. It doesn't matter if it takes you an hour to pick out a thought.

All that matters is that you start to clear these things from your mind, extract them from that cycle of overthinking, and get them down in the real world, where you can rationalise them.

Now, take a deep breath and write down *one* thing you can do to make each thing better, whether that's an action, or whether it's talking to somebody about the problem.

Now think: What if it all goes right?

Dear Human,

Is the thought of what could go wrong holding you back from doing something that you love? Have you thought about what could happen if it all went right?

It took us about two months before we finally picked up the courage to write our very first Instagram post, with some gentle nudging from our friend Doddz. He is one of the most creative people we know and, once we told him what we were planning, he literally forced us into doing it.

We were scared to express our feelings so openly in such a public space. We were scared that people would think we were stupid, that we'd do something wrong, or it just wouldn't take off.

We suspect we *never* considered in those months leading up to the first post, *What if it goes right*? Imagine if we hadn't started!

This doesn't have to just apply to business opportunities though. You can apply it to every single area of your life.

We guarantee this kind of worry is holding you back in far more places than you might think. For instance, do you ever think things like: What if I get fired for asking for a pay rise? I shouldn't get that dog I've wanted my entire life because I might be a bad dog owner.

The truth is our brains are programmed to be cautious. But if we're too cautious to try anything for fear of it going wrong, then we'll never truly get to live the life we want.

One of the beautiful things about starting Feel Good Club is that we've always been open and honest about the fact that we aren't, and have no desire to be, professionals.

We are simply encouraging and normalising a conversation around mental health and feelings in general.

We aren't perfect. We're still learning. And we definitely don't have all the answers. But when we post, it shows us, and others, that we aren't alone.

So, ask yourself . . . what if it all goes right?

TAKEAWAYS

1 A series of crappy situations don't mean your whole life is falling apart, but it's important not to deny your feelings in that moment, even if it's still going to be hard.

2 Say 'No' to toxic positivity. Things will go wrong and things will be hard, but things will also go right.

3 Write it down. Use a whole notepad or half a page. All that matters is that you get your worries out of your mind.

4 Stop asking what could go *wrong* and start asking what could go *right*.

2

Letting go of bad sh*t

Dear Human,

You are not obliged to hold on to things that make you feel bad.

Let go of the things you can't control, and the things you spend so much time worrying about.

We recommend a pinch of salt with this statement. We are by no means saying that it's easy to – or even that you should – just let go of your emotions, your trauma, or whatever it is that's causing you to worry right now.

But there are certain situations and times when recognising that some things are just out of our control can release us from a cycle of overthinking.

Kiera is a self-confessed control freak. She loves control, craves it, and spent a long time having a very hard time when she didn't have it.

And if you're like her, you've probably read that statement and laughed, because if she'd read that a couple of years ago, she'd have done the same.

However, after her struggles with an eating disorder, when she let her need for control take over her life, she finally realised that worrying about so many things had literally no impact on the outcome of the situation. For example:

- Being consumed by the thought of whether somebody likes you or not has literally no impact on their judgement of you.

- Being consumed by how someone will react to your boundaries has absolutely no control over how they will actually react.

- Being consumed by wondering whether it's going to rain tomorrow will not give you any control over the weather.

Eventually, we both came to realise that letting go of the thoughts and worries that may not happen, gives us more time and head space to deal with what's going on right now and, more importantly, enjoy what's going on right now.

If your head is clear of worry, you're less likely to care if somebody doesn't actually like you, are more equipped to deal with somebody's reaction to your boundaries, and you will probably remember to take an umbrella with you.

Rather than fixating on controlling the *outcome*, you can move forward and enjoy everything else in your life which then makes the outcome easier to deal with.

FEEL GOOD TIP

If you're struggling with overwhelming worries
and anxious thoughts, one way of trying to stop
them from constantly going around and around
in your mind could be starting a worry diary.
To do this, write your worries down, allowing
whatever comes to mind to flow out onto the
paper. Then, next to each worry, write down
the likelihood of each event happening. Ask
yourself if it's something you can control or
change. This can help you realise whether your
thoughts are rational or not and can bring you
some peace of mind.

STOP WORRYING ABOUT THE THINGS YOU CAN'T CONTROL AND START ENJOYING WHAT'S HAPPENING RIGHT NOW.

Dear Human,

Toxic relationships aren't always romantic ones. They can be with family or friends, in work places or non-professional situations. They can even arise from your relationship with yourself.

And just because the relationship is toxic, it doesn't always mean that the people involved are toxic – although sometimes it does!

Removing yourself from a toxic relationship, or a toxic situation, is one of the greatest forms of self-care. If you have ever done it, or are planning to, you should be ridiculously proud of yourself, because it's hard.

It's easy to think that just because a situation is toxic that it must be easy to remove yourself from it, that you won't feel pain or be hurt because of it, but that couldn't be further from the truth. The more toxic the relationship, the harder it usually is to leave.

We can't leave that thought behind without telling you that that's okay. It's okay that it's hard to leave, and it's okay that you're going to mourn the relationship. It's normal and you are definitely not alone . . . but you have to realise that you deserve better.

THE MORE TOXIC THE RELATIONSHIP, THE HARDER IT USUALLY IS TO LEAVE.

Throughout our life, and especially in our first year of business, we lost friends that we had thought would be there for the longhaul. At the time we were really upset about it, but eventually realised that sometimes people change, that some friendships serve different purposes at different times in one's life, and that sometimes it's better to walk away when things are no longer the same.

It's also important to note that just because a relationship might turn toxic, it doesn't discredit the good times you had together while it lasted although ultimately this makes it more upsetting when it ends.

It's really hard owning a business, especially given that our first year was during a global pandemic. And during this time, we weren't the best friends, or the best daughters, best aunties, or even the best wives to each other, because at that time our priority was just getting through the year.

THE PEOPLE WHO STICK BY YOU DURING DIFFICULT TIMES ARE YOUR TRUE CIRCLE OF FRIENDS.

The people who stick by you during difficult times are your true circle of friends. Some relationships we keep because they are comfortable, or because we don't want to upset the person concerned. But we're only here once, so live life with people who uplift you, people who cheer you on, people who will wait weeks for a reply and are still happy to hear from you when you do get in touch.

LIVE LIFE WITH PEOPLE WHO UPLIFT YOU, PEOPLE WHO CHEER YOU ON.

Dear Human,

We are aware that things that have happened to us in our past can, and do, have huge impacts on all aspects of our life.

The previous statement aims to work as a little reminder that, as humans, we are constantly evolving, changing, and growing. If you made mistakes, did things you're not proud of, then you're not alone. It's okay to make peace with that, to forgive yourself, and to move forward.

The person you were in your past doesn't define you now.

THE PERSON YOU WERE IN YOUR PAST DOESN'T DEFINE YOU NOW.

Dear Human,

We're all for challenging ourselves, for raising the bar, and getting out of our comfort zone, but it's important to remember that we aren't always going to meet those expectations. We're human and we need patience, especially from ourselves. If we are consistently raising the bar too high and expecting something unrealistic of ourselves, we will set ourselves up for failure by creating a cycle of self-doubt.

It's important to recognise that your goals, needs, passions, and desires will change. Is it fair to hold yourself to getting top marks in something if, a year into it, you realise it's not for you?

Can we really expect to be motivated and passionate about something that no longer aligns with us?

Be intentional about your goals. Make it a habit to check in and ask yourself whether your goals are still relevant, and stop putting unrealistic expectations on yourself.

FEEL GOOD TIP

Start working on your boundaries and take note of the relationships that lift you up the most and make a conscious effort to surround yourself with those people more often.

STOP PUTTING

UNREALISTIC

EXPECTATIONS

ON YOURSELF.

TAKEAWAYS

1 A relationship ending doesn't always eradicate a happy past together.

2 Be realistic with your goals, don't keep raising the bar without raising the level of patience and care you give to yourself.

3 You don't need to be liked by everybody you meet, just as you won't like everyone you come into contact with.

4 Like any relationship, romantic or not, you need to remember to continually work on and nurture the relationship you have with yourself.

3

Your happiness above everything

MENU

- Putting yourself first
- FOMO (Fear Of Missing Out) vs. JOMO (Joy Of Missing Out)
- Saying 'No'
- Boundaries
- Reconnecting with what you love

Dear Human,

We all have responsibilities, and although there are some situations where we just 'gotta do what we gotta do', there are many others whereby we neglect to put our own happiness and our needs first.

As a daft example of the above, when our dog Juno decides she wants a wee at 4.30 a.m., even though we made it very clear to her at 10 p.m. that that was her final chance to have one, and that if she barked for one in the night, she'd have to hold it in. Of course we don't really mean that. We stumble down the stairs and stand shivering at the back door while she sniffs every blade of grass before finally coming back in.

Does that make us happy? No.

Would putting our happiness first mean staying fast asleep in our warm bed? Yes.

But as we said, sometimes you've just gotta do what you've gotta do.

PUT YOUR OWN HAPPINESS AND NEEDS FIRST.

Dear Human,

You've probably heard of FOMO (Fear Of Missing Out), but have you heard of JOMO (Joy Of Missing Out)? This is the feeling you get when you say 'No' to something you really don't want to do, and instead spend your time doing exactly what makes you feel good.

We'd like to know when FOMO became a thing. It's probably always been a thing, but we can't imagine Aimie's grandma suffering from as much FOMO when her mates are at bingo and she's decided to stay in and read a book as we do when our friends go out but we stay home. And this is probably because she doesn't use social media.

We have the lives of everybody we care about at our fingertips, on a screen, and to add a tiny bit more pressure, we also have the lives of celebrities and influencers whose jobs it is to reveal how much fun they are having, at a certain place, in a certain outfit.

When we can click a button and watch every bit of the night out we *could* have been on, it makes it much harder to prioritise our own needs, a life-admin day, or the relaxed evening we so desperately need. We can see what others had for lunch, what bar they're going to next, and witness a warped view of how much fun we're missing out on.

DON'T LET FOMO BE A REASON TO NEGLECT YOUR OWN NEEDS.

We're definitely not saying that sharing what
we're doing and having fun can't go hand in hand,
but let's be honest, we're only really sharing the
best bits, even if we are experiencing them through
a phone.

Our checklist to combatting FOMO consists of
asking ourselves the following questions:

1   Do we actually want to go, or do we just want
    to share it on social media?

2   Is this going to make us happy?

3   Do we want to be there?

4   Do we have the energy for this right now?

5   Do we need to prioritise something else?

FEEL GOOD TIP

Create your own FOMO checklist.

Just remember that if you don't have the energy for those weekend plans, you're allowed to stay home. Don't let your fear of missing out be a reason to neglect your own needs.

Dear Human,

Unless someone's paying you and
it's literally in your job description,
it is not your job to please anybody.

Maybe we're being a little dramatic here, but it's important to get the point across. If you're in a loving and healthy relationship, or you're a parent, there are times when you will naturally want to please other people, but the key thing here is *wanting to*.

Beyond this you are not obligated to please other people, especially when it happens to be to the detriment of your own happiness.

Deep down, we're all people-pleasers, we're human, and we have an inherent need to be liked. But there's a difference between being a good person and putting yourself second in every single situation just to please someone else.

It's not your job to please everybody, so stop saying 'Yes' when you mean 'No'.

STOP SAYING 'YES' WHEN YOU MEAN 'NO'.

We have both always struggled with people-pleasing in our personal lives and in our working lives. We'd overwork, feeling unable to say 'No' at the thought of letting somebody down. And when it came to the weekend, we'd fill our days and evenings with lots of plans, agree to everything and, ultimately, let people down. If you haven't guessed the outcome of this, it was a hefty case of burnout and a constant cycle of feeling like a bad friend.

Our takeaway from this was that the world doesn't stop if you don't answer that email after 6 p.m. and leave it until the next morning. Your friends won't hate you for not making that Sunday morning coffee.

What is in your control is how you deal with these things. By having boundaries, you avoid over-agreeing and underdelivering. You save your energy for the things that really bring you joy, and when your cup is full, you can share that with the people and things you love.

BY HAVING BOUNDARIES YOU AVOID OVER-AGREEING AND UNDERDELIVERING.

Our people-pleasing and inability to say 'No' definitely intensified when we started Feel Good Club. We were so overwhelmed with the positive response we had to the brand that we felt like we needed to agree to every opportunity that presented itself. After a while we quickly learnt that we couldn't please everybody, and not everything that was presented to us aligned with us as people or with our brand.

We're not going to pretend that it's easy, or that once you start putting boundaries in place, or saying 'No', you're magically able to maintain this course of action. We had – and still have – sleepless nights about saying 'No' to the energy-drink supplier that wanted to be stocked in the club, and not closing the space for a kitten's first birthday party. Although we're a team of animal lovers, and would probably have enjoyed it, it just wasn't possible . . . and Juno, our coffee shop dog, would not have been very happy!

'Boundaries' has become a bit of a buzz word, but it isn't a new concept that we need to apply immediately to our lives and announce to the world in order to be happy. Having boundaries simply means understanding what you do, or don't align with, what you are, and aren't comfortable with, and allowing yourself to communicate that to others without feeling guilty about it.

Always try to remember that by clearly communicating your boundaries as soon as possible in a situation that doesn't work for you, you're saving yourself a lot of worry and hassle in the long run, because when we don't express our limits, we can find ourselves in a situation where we have to back-track on what we've done, said, or agreed to, and end up feeling bad.

COMMUNICATE YOUR BOUNDARIES AS SOON AS POSSIBLE.

For instance, the time Kiera didn't correct somebody who thought she was Ellie Goulding in a club in Portugal many years ago. Within twenty minutes, she found herself in the VIP area with six crates of Budweiser, before being pulled up onto the stage to sing 'Starry Eyes' and then ushered to the back for a group photo with the whole team. In this book, she'd like to formally apologise to that club for not communicating clearly that she wasn't in fact Ellie Goulding – she just didn't want to let the excited team member down by saying 'No'.

Dear Human,

We've had so many conversations with various therapists that always start with us feeling like there's something wrong with us, for not knowing what makes us feel good, or what we enjoy anymore.

After talking to somebody about this, we realised we're actually not weird for feeling this way and that we're not alone either.

Sometimes, life takes over and we have to make time to reconnect with what we love.

We found this especially true when we reached our mid to late twenties. At this point, life usually begins to feel serious: we have more responsibilities that take up the energy we usually give to the things we love. It becomes harder to meet people and we also have less time to socialise.

We created the physical space of Feel Good Club with the aim of reminding people to reconnect with themselves. We hold regular events to inspire and bring people together, from spoken word to live music gigs, workshops, art, and 'Feel Good Friends', which is essentially speed dating, but to meet and make friends in a safe space.

Even though life can, and will, take over at times, in order to enjoy our day-to-day we must make a conscious effort to make time to figure out what makes us feel good – because that will change over time! – and prioritise this when and where we can.

FEEL GOOD TIP

Use this time, right now, to list five things that make you feel good and that you'd like to do more of.

Finding what makes us feel good doesn't always come naturally. Give yourself time to reconnect with what you love.

Do more of what makes you feel good and less of what doesn't.

It doesn't need to make sense; it just needs to feel good.

DO MORE OF WHAT MAKES YOU FEEL GOOD AND LESS OF WHAT DOESN'T.

TAKEAWAYS

1 If something doesn't align with your values, you're allowed to say 'No', and so are other people.

2 It's okay to communicate your boundaries.

3 Missing out on things isn't always a bad thing, embrace your JOMO.

4

Overthinking

MENU

- Perspective
- Don't believe your thoughts
- Beer Fear
- Talk to someone

Dear Human,

We don't think there's a person on this plane that can honestly say they have never suffered from overthinking. If there is, we'd love to know their secret.

Although we can't give you a cure for your poor overthinking mind, we can tell you that you're not alone, and give you some advice on how to manage your overthinking, so that it doesn't become all-consuming.

As always, please remember that we are only speaking from lived experience here. What works for us might not work for you, but there is absolutely no harm in trying, hey?

If you're thinking it or feeling it, it's valid. Yes, some of the things you overthink might actually be silly when you say them out loud – like our constant worry that our dog doesn't love us! – but that doesn't make you silly for thinking them in the first place.

PERSPECTIVE
IS
EVERYTHING.

Perspective really is everything, but if we're overthinking it can be ridiculously difficult to see things clearly and, once you're in a hole, it's far easier to keep digging your way to the bottom than climb up to the top. Thoughts, words, and flashbacks of what you said or did fall on you each time you try to get out.

Aimie suffers from overthinking pretty often. She'll overthink about money – a very valid thing by the way! – or about not texting somebody back straightaway, not laughing hard enough at somebody's joke . . . She even worries about asking for the bill in a restaurant because she doesn't want to disturb the waiting staff.

Aimie overthinks so much that she thinks paying for something – a legal requirement, and something that could land her in jail if she didn't do it – might disturb somebody.

All jokes aside though, this is an issue she works on every day, and something that helps her break her cycle of overthinking is thinking in 10s.

She asks herself: Will this matter in 10 minutes, 10 days, 10 weeks? How about 10 months? What about 10 years?

For Aimie, this helps her to realise that actually the thing that is all-consuming right now she won't give a second thought in a couple of weeks – and that puts it into perspective.

How many times have you had sleepless nights over something only for it to never materialise? Sleep is far too important to lose out on for something that won't matter next week.

FEEL GOOD TIP

Try and interrupt the cycle of overthinking and find some perspective by asking yourself out loud, or on paper: Is this going to matter next week?

Try and interrupt the cycle of overthinking and find some perspective.

Dear Human,

*Does your brain think about all this stuff
that probably won't happen, and leave it up
to you to figure out if it's real or irrational?
Don't believe everything you think.*

Bizarrely, our good friend the brain can make us believe we are sh*t. For example, you think you left the front door unlocked again, so you need to go back and check it, or that your whole friendship group hates you because you missed a message in the group chat, and now everyone has discovered what a terrible friend you are.

How many times has that happened and you've accepted that it's 100 per cent true? We've lost count how many times that's happened to us. When you finally open up about it and realise that nobody noticed anyway, then you probably start overthinking the fact that you're so unnoticeable.

When Aimie overthinks, the majority of the things that she overthinks are actually quite sensible.

The things Kiera overthinks, on the other hand, are things that will probably never happen. Kiera can't believe she's sharing these thoughts, but if she can share them in this book with hopefully what will be *millions* of readers, then you can share your thoughts too.

OUR GOOD FRIEND THE BRAIN CAN MAKE US BELIEVE WE ARE SH*T.

So, for example, she thinks:

- Every time we take Juno for a walk a wild horse will appear and attack us.

- That an animal might escape from the zoo (not that we live near one) and that might attack us too. She spends the whole walk on guard, ready to protect our family.

- Every time we go on water, whether it's in a boat, a pedalo, or a kayak, Kiera is convinced she'll be eaten by a shark. It wouldn't be so bad if she'd actually been to countries that *have* dangerous sharks.

Kiera was also convinced for the majority of her life that if she ate a kidney bean she'd be poisoned and die! It was only when we made a chilli dish at Feel Good Club and she announced in front of the team that she didn't want to put kidney beans in it in case we made someone poorly, that she finally realised how irrational her thinking was.

She's since eaten one or two, but still isn't quite comfortable with it.

Kiera could literally write pages of her irrational thoughts and the ridiculous things her brain conjures up as she's falling asleep. It's actually quite entertaining at times, but she's now learnt to say what she's thinking and laugh about it instead of actually letting these things worry her.

Maybe your thoughts are as extreme as hers or maybe they aren't. Either way, without practice, it can be really difficult to rationalise our thoughts, and irrational thoughts are actually your brain's way of trying to prepare you for an outcome, by making the unknown less scary should it happen.

So how can we start to rationalise our thoughts? There are two options:

1 You can be like Kiera and say them out loud, let everyone laugh at you, laugh at yourself, and be entertained by the ridiculous stuff that pops into your brain, or

2 You can grab your notepad and challenge the irrational thought.

FEEL GOOD TIP

Write down *why* you had irrational thoughts. For instance:

- What you were doing at the time?

- What did you actually believe at the time? That is, what did you think was going to happen? And how did that belief make you feel?

You can then start to recognise any unhelpful thinking styles and patterns.

The next time you're overthinking what you said to somebody, consider that they are probably overthinking what they said to you too.

Irrational thoughts are your brain's way of trying to prepare you for an outcome, by making the unknown less scary.

Dear Human,

Have you considered that we're all probably spending the majority of our time overthinking what we might have said to each other instead of what the other person actually said?

This one used to be a biggie for Kiera, especially when she used to drink. 'Beer Fear' used to hit hard and she'd spend days wondering who she'd offended and what she'd said to somebody.

At the time of writing this book, Kiera has been alcohol-free for several months and can't believe how much this kind of overthinking has lessened and consequently improved.

We're not saying that the answer is to stop drinking, because not everybody needs to. It's simply what's working for Kiera. But what we have noticed is that many of our friends, when hungover, have messaged us to ask if they've misbehaved, or if they've said anything stupid, and then have admitted that they have, 'The worst *Beer Fear* in the world.'

At the time, Kiera could barely even tell that our friends were drunk, so now makes sure to let her friends know that their overthinking is probably caused by Beer Fear.

Dear Human,

You are not a burden for talking about how you feel.

TALK TO A LOVED ONE, TO SOMEBODY YOU TRUST.

Being in a cycle of overthinking is one of the loneliest places in the world, but you're not alone and you can talk about it.

Don't underestimate how much of an impact being in a cycle of overthinking can have on your mental and physical health. When you're in it, the time can seem to fly past. You end up functioning on autopilot and it's easy for your relationships to break down around you, because you become withdrawn and distant.

This is your reminder to talk about it – a reminder that you don't have to do this alone.

You can talk to a loved one, to somebody you trust, or a quick Google search will bring up a number of incredible charities you can reach out to, if you feel like you have nobody to talk to.

Know that whatever it is, it will get better.

KNOW THAT WHATEVER IT IS, IT WILL GET BETTER.

TAKEAWAYS

1 Try the 10s method and see if it works for you.

2 Get into the habit of writing down your thoughts to help rationalise them.

3 Try and talk about how you feel and what you're overthinking without feeling 'silly'.

5

Being proud of yourself

MENU

- Getting through the hardest days

- Being you

- Valuing others

- Take a rest

- Work-Life Balance

Dear Human,

Why do we find it so hard, dare we say it, even cringe-worthy, to admit that we're proud of ourselves? Why do we find it so difficult to shout about our achievements, especially when they are so worthy of praise? It's okay to be proud of yourself. You should be your own biggest cheerleader. You don't need the approval of anybody else to be proud of yourself.

Let go of the idea that you have to do something life-changing or extraordinary to be proud of yourself. Simply getting through a bad day is reason enough. You've made it through all your bad days so far and you can do it again.

Time and time again we have conversations with people who say they have nothing to be proud of, they just can't find a reason. If you came into this chapter thinking the same, we want to tell you that you have so many reasons to be proud of yourself.

One of the biggest reasons to be proud of yourself is probably one of the easiest ones to disregard – getting through your hardest days. What is there not to be proud of here? You've managed to carry yourself through your darkest days, when you felt like there was no way out.

Take a second to reflect:

● Can you remember the last time you felt like things just wouldn't or couldn't get better?

● Did you get through it?

● Can you remember how hard you fought every single day to get to where you are now?

YOU'VE MADE IT THROUGH ALL YOUR BAD DAYS SO FAR AND YOU CAN DO IT AGAIN.

BEING PROUD OF YOURSELF

When Kiera was in the depths of her eating disorder, she felt like life would never feel normal again. During the early stages of her recovery, she forgot one crucial part – to celebrate and be proud of herself for each day that she made a step forward.

It's actually only recently that she realised and acknowledged how proud she should be for getting through those days, and today we challenge you to do the same.

There is literally only one of you in the entire world; your life, your skills, your experiences, and the way you show love are all unique to you. These are all things to be proud of.

Dear Human,

There was a 1 in 400 trillion chance of you being born. How incredible is that?

It's so easy to get caught up in watching other people's success, watching their lives play out from afar, watching them achieve their goals and, in some cases, watching them do the things that you wish you were doing. This is a perfect recipe for destructive comparisons and neglecting to be proud of yourself for the steps that you're taking, which should encourage you to continue moving forward.

But nobody else is *you*. Nobody else has lived your experiences. Nobody has the same skills or uses them in same way that you do. Nobody else shows love and friendship like you do. And the more you acknowledge that, the greater your sense of self-worth becomes.

When we first opened Feel Good Club, we worried that people wouldn't understand what we were trying to do, that as we had no experience people would choose the more established coffee shops, brunch spots, or bars over ours. These thoughts and worries took over the fact that we should have actually been extremely proud of what we'd achieved.

NOBODY ELSE IS *YOU*. THE MORE YOU ACKNOWLEDGE THAT, THE GREATER YOUR SENSE OF SELF-WORTH BECOMES.

Eventually, we realised that although we might be similar in some ways to various other spaces, nobody else was *us*, just like nobody was *them*. And this realisation helped us get through some especially difficult times during the pandemic.

FEEL GOOD TIP

With this in mind, and without sounding like teachers, we're going to set you some homework. Make a list of all the things you're proud of and another list of all the things that make you *you*. Spend some time reflecting on them each day this week and we guarantee there will be an improvement in the way you speak to yourself.

By just being yourself, you make somebody else's day and life better. You inspire them. You make them smile. They wouldn't want to be without you . . . even if you don't realise it.

By just being yourself, you make somebody else's day and life better.

Dear Human,

Just because people don't always let you know it, doesn't mean that you're not valued, that you're not a great friend, and that by simply existing, you're making somebody's day better.

It's funny, isn't it, that we have people in our lives that we see most days – they could be our family, partners, friends, colleagues – and our day just wouldn't be the same without them.

Tell your friends how much you value simply being around them and, in turn, be proud of yourself for the person you are to them.

TELL YOUR FRIENDS HOW MUCH YOU VALUE THEM.

Dear Human,

*Normalise being proud of giving your body
what it needs, especially if that need is rest.*

So, you've started your day, whatever point you're at now. The day has started and you are, at the least, awake. Whatever you're doing right now, you're doing it for you, because you're reading this very book. And that's a choice you've made for yourself.

We wrote an Instagram post recently that said, 'Praise me when I'm healthy, not when I'm burnt out and ill', because we often get the most praise in our life when we are struggling the most, because we throw ourselves into work and projects and don't look after ourselves.

That is not the way things should be. We should want praise when we've got a healthy work-life balance, when we're enjoying our life, when we have healthy relationships with the people and things around us.

We should want praise when we've got a healthy work-life balance.

We're guilty of doing it too in the past: praising somebody for clearly burning themselves out, telling them they're smashing their business, and forcing ourselves to work harder too because we thought that was the way to get more praise.

But we're learning to be mindful about that and tend to tell our friends to stop working so hard a lot more.

When we started out in hospitality, we were shocked to see how ingrained it is in the industry for people to not take breaks. To be honest, it's been the same in many places we've worked, but hospitality is really hard work, with long hours and being on your feet all day long, serving other people before yourself.

At Feel Good Club there is a 'must-have-a-break' policy and if anyone tries to skip their break, they are told off! A healthy and happy team is a well-rested one so there's no burnout-praise culture allowed!

TAKEAWAYS

1 Stop what you're doing right now and think of one reason that you're proud of yourself today.

2 Grab some paper, and do the Feel Good Tip from this chapter.

3 Message a friend right now and let them know that you're proud of them, and why.

6

Don't compare yourself with others

MENU

- Life is not a competition

- Being different

- Things are not always as they seem

- Journey vs. destination

Dear Human,

We really need you to stop comparing your life to everybody else's. We need you to stop comparing your body, your job, your relationships, and everything else to the best bits other people choose to share with you.

Everything in life fluctuates – our mood and motivation included. Don't expect to be able to give the same energy consistently.

Consider the saying: 'The only comparison you should make is between who you were yesterday and who you are today.'

However, we disagree with this statement. Yesterday we were living our best life: it was the weekend, we had free time and spent it with the people we love. Today, we're having a mini breakdown, everything's going wrong, and we don't feel like we have the energy to get out of bed.

In all honesty, comparing our best self to our worst self makes us feel like sh*t and makes us think: *Why can't we just be that person all the time?*

The truth is, we can't. Every single thing in our lives fluctuates on a more regular basis than we think, including our mood, our weight, our mental health, and so on.

Be patient with yourself and make no comparisons, even with yourself.

It's not a competition. We're all going at our own pace, in our own way, and that's okay.

BE PATIENT WITH YOURSELF AND MAKE NO COMPARISONS.

Dear Human,

We're not here to live our life in competition with anybody else. Your life is yours to live. By comparing every aspect of it to other people's lifestyles, we're constantly putting ourselves down, which contributes to that negative self-talk spiral you might find yourself in when you're having a particularly hard time with comparisons.

Growing up we are taught so many harmful things that encourage this competitive comparison loop. We're told what we should do with our lives based on our education, told that we should be able to buy a house by a certain age, that we should get married and have children.

But none of these things we're taught as children take into account our financial circumstances; the current housing market; the fact that not everyone is able – or wants – to have children; that queer people exist (and should be celebrated, for that matter), and may not wish, or be keen, to follow the *traditional* marriage or relationship path.

The one thing we should be told is that *our* goals aren't for everyone. No two people are the same and that's a beautiful thing, so let's stop putting pressure on ourselves to conform to an outdated idea of what life should be like, in order for our life to be deemed successful.

Throughout our journey with Feel Good Club, we've never seen other people, businesses, or clothing brands as competition.

YOUR GOALS AREN'T FOR EVERYONE. NO TWO PEOPLE ARE THE SAME.

We've always viewed others doing something similar to us as an inspiration. Likewise, seeing people and businesses doing something totally different from us is also energising. We shop at other independents, eat in their establishments, go to their events, and we give each other advice, as we believe that it's far better to make uplifting connections with people than to see them as competitors.

At the club we host events, we sell other people's food and bakes, and sell people's art work. The more we can inspire each other, the better the world will be. We constantly remind ourselves that without the help and generosity of other people we absolutely would not be doing this today and that's something we always try to give back to others.

Like we said earlier, *No one is you!* Rather than focusing on competition, let's focus on being our best and happiest self – and loving the not-so-best or less-happy versions.

Stop comparing your everyday to somebody else's best bits.

STOP COMPARING YOUR EVERYDAY TO SOMEBODY ELSE'S BEST BITS.

Dear Human,

The person behind the post isn't always as happy as they might seem in their story.

DON'T COMPARE YOURSELF WITH OTHERS

We all have mundane things to do on a daily basis, like remembering to drink water, tie our shoelaces and clip our nails. But why is it unhealthy to compare the everyday and mundane to the best bits that people curate and choose to share on social media?

The latter is what social media was created for. Of course, many people use it as an incredibly important and beneficial tool, to raise awareness and spread positivity, but many of us use it as a way to record and document the best and most enjoyable moments of our lives.

There is absolutely nothing wrong with that. Remember when we had film cameras? No one put the accidental shot of their foot in the photo album. And most people probably took all the bad pictures out of the packet before passing the photos around the dinner table.

It is definitely *not* a bad thing to share our highlights online. Keep doing it. Celebrate your achievements. Post your favourite holiday pictures, the fancy restaurant you might never go to again. Post it all – and don't feel bad about it.

But . . . when we're on the receiving end of those images, we forget that we don't post the picture of our holiday blues, when it takes us three weeks to unpack our cases (yes, that's Kiera!). We forget that we didn't post the pictures of the beans on toast we ate for a week after spending too much at the fancy restaurant.

Yet it's so easy for us to compare our mundane moments to those more exciting snippets.

What's even more damaging is that these curated posts actually make other moments feel far more mundane than they are, and makes us ungrateful for them when in actual fact, some of them are our favourite moments.

Of course, we aren't going to be grateful all the time. Sometimes we're on autopilot, but it's important to consciously try and take note of the little things more often.

Be grateful you get to put your socks on each day. Be grateful that you've got toast to butter. Beans on toast is actually one of our favourite meals ever. And just this morning as we were getting ready for work, Aimie said, 'Isn't it amazing that we are going to work for ourselves, and that the business we work for is what pays our mortgage?' We were both excited at the thought of that.

We're always very honest about the fact that neither Aimie or I come from money. Like we said in the Introduction, we only had an unexpected £500 refund to invest in the business ourselves. People assume that because we have a business, over 300,000 followers, and a physical space that we must be made of money, when it's really not the case. This is yet another harmful comparison and assumption based on what people see on social media.

FEEL GOOD TIP

It's time to practice more gratitude. We started a Gratitude Journal but Kiera has a hard time sticking to things like this. If you do too, maybe you could try what Aimie does: most mornings she sets a reminder to ask what we're both grateful for before we leave the house. It's a great way to start the day by feeling good about what *you* have and what *you're* doing, rather than focusing on other people.

We wanted to end this section with a reminder to check on your friends, even if they seem like they're living their best life according to their Instagram, because everything isn't always as it seems behind the screen. Sometimes when things are getting tough, it's easy to overshare things that make it look like you're doing fine when, in reality, you're withdrawing.

Stop comparing your starting point to somebody else's end goal. If you focus too much on where you need to be next, you'll miss the best part: the journey.

STOP COMPARING YOUR STARTING POINT TO SOMEBODY ELSE'S END GOAL.

Dear Human,

The destination will never feel as good as you think it will, it's the bits along the way where the real joy happens.

If you have asked anyone who has achieved a goal whether they are satisfied, we have a sneaking suspicion that they will probably always want to go that little bit further. It doesn't even have to be their 'end goal', because is there really ever an 'end goal'? Our values, feelings and desires change over time and that's fine. It's actually more than fine to want to keep moving forward and increase your happiness. If you ask anyone who's ever achieved a goal (yourself included), they will probably tell you that the best bit was the lead-up to it.

Of course, the day we opened Feel Good Club was great and our gratitude level was sky high, but even better was:

● The evening we spent jumping around the front room after we'd got an absolute bargain on Gumtree and paid £100 for all our café chairs and tables – big love to Prufrock Coffee in London who helped a fellow independent more than they know!

- The week before opening, when everything was set up, and we ate Deliveroo by candlelight.

- Telling our friends and family that it was actually going to happen.

- The trips to IKEA.

- Hiring our team, which enabled us to meet two of our best friends in the entire world. Tash, who took the first ever photos of our clothing line before they were even on sale, eventually joined the business to grow our content and events. She has given us so much support and was the person who truly believed in us from day one. The business now wouldn't be the same without her unbelievable creative mind. And Jess, who has been there throughout the physical space journey, picked us up when we've been at rock bottom, helped us to grow the business and create our vision, as well as form a beautiful friendship.

We can remember the day we realised that we'd spent the last year or so comparing our starting point to other people's completed goal and wrote an Instagram post about it. It resonated with so many people, and made us realise we definitely aren't alone in this and that this pointless exercise is far more common than we'd thought.

But let's break it down. You decide to buy a house and start saving. On Instagram you might see your friends buying houses and feel deflated, but unless they were fortunate enough to have support with buying theirs, they've probably gone through a similar journey of saving up for it. You're comparing your starting point – the first £1 saved or spent – to somebody else who has done that and has now achieved their goal.

When Aimie first quit her job to start working on establishing Feel Good Club, our very good friend, Steven Bartlett, kindly gave her a mentoring session. We both remember the advice he gave her. He told her to enjoy the small wins because when you get to the big ones, it'll always be an anticlimax, there's no brass band waiting at the end, the world isn't waiting to clap for you, and he told her not to focus on the end goal.

MAKE A POINT OF BEING AWARE OF, AND ENJOYING, PERSONAL GOALS.

So, we've always made a point of consciously being aware of, and enjoying, the more personal goals, being able to expand and grow our team, getting out of our comfort zone, hitting our daily target (this doesn't happen every day!), meeting someone new who inspires us, or just simply getting out of bed and looking forward to our day.

TAKEAWAYS

1 Be patient with yourself.

2 Don't compare yourself to others. Acknowledge the competition, lift each other up, and inspire each other.

3 Gratitude doesn't need to be saved for the huge milestones or moments, you can find it in the everyday.

4 Don't focus so much on the end goal, and celebrate the mini wins.

7

When you're struggling

Dear Human,

Earlier we touched on toxic positivity and how damaging that can be, especially when we're struggling. It's probably been ingrained into most of us, for most of our lives, without us even realising.

We can all probably remember countless times that we've been told to 'Cheer up' or not to 'Put a downer' on situations when we just aren't feeling ourselves. There have probably been thousands of instances like this in everyone's life, which have caused us to struggle with feeling that we need to be positive all the time.

Having a positive outlook on life can be incredible for our overall wellbeing, but the reality is that life isn't always positive. Our experiences are all relative to us and they can be painful. So, it's important that we feel, talk about, and process them.

Having a positive outlook on life can be incredible for our overall wellbeing.

You've probably been affected by toxic positivity if you've ever:

1 Felt guilty about being upset, angry or hurt.

2 Ignored your problems, especially by thinking: *This isn't serious enough for me to be upset about.*

3 Been told, told somebody else, or told yourself, to 'Look on the bright side.'

4 Hidden how you really feel because you're worried someone might think you're being negative.

PRETENDING TO BE OKAY TAKES UP FAR MORE ENERGY THAN TALKING ABOUT HOW YOU'RE FEELING.

And if you have been affected by toxic positivity, or displayed any of the above behaviours to other people, please don't start feeling like a bad person. As we said, so many of us have been conditioned to think this way, but it's time to learn that having a bad day is absolutely normal and that however you feel is okay.

Pretending to be okay takes up far more energy than talking about how you're feeling.

FEEL GOOD TIP

Next time you're feeling particularly low, don't try and hide it, instead, talk to somebody you trust and be open about exactly how you're feeling. No matter how big or small the situation is.

Dear Human,

Starting to process painful situations begins with allowing yourself to feel down in the first place.

Unclench that jaw, roll your shoulders, and let the weight you're carrying start to drop off.

Most people would rather do a 12-hour shift on their feet than spend twelve hours in their head holding onto something painful and pretending to be okay. It's exhausting and unhealthy, and it will make you physically and mentally unwell.

How many times have you spent hours, days, maybe even weeks, trying to hide how you feel, only to finally open up and wonder why you didn't do it straight away? It's okay that we do this. We're human and sometimes we forget that we're allowed to talk about how we feel. Sometimes our minds play tricks on us and tell us we'll be a burden for opening up. But this is a little prompt reminding you that you're not.

Say how you feel, say what's on your mind, what you're worried about, what you love, and what you don't. It'll give you far more energy to focus on the things that matter.

We're human and sometimes we forget that we're allowed to talk about how we feel.

Dear Human,

Yes, other people's words and actions can affect you in many ways, but we want you to know that how they make you feel about yourself is not your fault – it's a reflection on them and not you.

YOU ARE NOT ALL THE SH*TTY THINGS SOMEBODY HAS SAID OR DONE TO YOU.

WHEN YOU'RE STRUGGLING

You're not defined by all the sh*tty things someone has said or done to you.

Read that again.

Read that five times over.

In fact, fold down the corner of this page and open it every time you feel differently.

This world wouldn't be the same without you.

You make a difference every single day, even on the days when you struggle to see what that difference is.

You're here and we're glad that you are.

The world is a better place with you in it and it always will be.

No matter how low you might feel right now, this feeling won't last forever.

We need you to read that sentence out loud, and we need you to believe it when you say it, because it's true.

This feeling isn't going to last forever. Whatever it is that you're experiencing right now, things will get better. And we know this because we've been there, and they always do.

Remember all the times that the crushing feeling felt like it'd be with you forever? Like your first heartbreak – and your second, third, fourth, fifth . . . It doesn't get easier, does it? Being dumped feels as if nothing will ever be the same again; a pain so strong that is only slightly soothed by listening to Adele on repeat for hours on end.

When we broke up, after a year of being together, Aimie's housemates had to enforce a house-wide Adele ban, and she's very open about the fact that she spent a good six months thinking that her single shot at love was over, and she'd never be happy again.

WHATEVER IT IS THAT YOU'RE EXPERIENCING RIGHT NOW, THINGS WILL GET BETTER.

How many times have we all been there?
We can't speak for everyone, but there is a very
good chance that you will move on and find love
again. The heartbreak might even make you a
stronger person.

A year later, Aimie was stronger than ever and
Kiera had to beg her to take her back.

Stop putting pressure on yourself to get over it.
Feel the feelings. There's a reason they are there.

Dear Human,

You are not a burden for needing to talk about your mental health or about how you feel, and if anyone ever makes you feel like that, then they aren't the kind of person that deserves to be in your life.

YOU ARE NOT A BURDEN FOR TALKING ABOUT YOUR MENTAL HEALTH OR ABOUT HOW YOU FEEL.

One of the main reasons we started Feel Good Club was to normalise the conversation around mental health and not only mental health. We wanted to normalise talking about how we *feel*.

You don't have to suffer with your mental health or have a diagnosis to struggle. It's important to remember that we all have *mental* health in the same way that we all have *physical* health. Many people associate the words 'mental health' with a diagnosis. But it's a constant, it's always there, it concerns the health of our mind and how we feel and, some days, that's going to be better than others. Like we've said before, everything fluctuates and talking about those fluctuations can help keep our mind healthy.

TAKEAWAY

1 **You are not a burden for talking about how you feel. That is all.**

8

Don't feel guilty

Dear Human,

Let's talk about guilt. It's a normal human emotion: feeling guilty for making a mistake, for upsetting your friend, for hurting your partner or somebody you care about, for leaving somebody on read.

Don't feel
guilty for
prioritising
you and your
happiness.

Guilt is normal and, in many situations, we *should* feel guilty and use that guilt to learn how we can be better when we make a mistake, to make changes so we avoid hurting people again. However, there are so many situations and occasions where we feel guilty for something that we really don't need to, and that's not good for us. For example, having two takeaways in a row, or being too poorly to go to work.

You are the only person that's totally and completely responsible for your own happiness and you need to be able to prioritise this without feeling guilty.

As we've said before – and we know we're repeating ourselves here! – we need to be able to say 'No' to taking on extra work if we don't have the energy and it's going to make us unhappy. We need to be able to say 'No' to that last minute 'Are you free to chat?' call if we're just about to get in the bath because we've had a long, hard and sh*tty day. We need to be able to say 'No' to going out for our friend's sister's cousin's brother's birthday if we really don't want to go. And we need to say 'No' without feeling guilty about it.

Because guess what? A lot of the time, guilt makes us say 'Yes', when we actually mean 'No'. Then, at the last minute, we'll probably cancel, so our friend and their sister's cousin's brother will be annoyed with us, and then we'll have a reason to actually feel guilty.

So, the moral of this story, my friends, is to say 'No' without feeling guilty, because otherwise you'll probably end up with a real reason to feel that way.

Don't feel guilty for saying 'No' to things that don't align with you.

You don't have to feel guilty about other people's reactions to your boundaries – it says more about them than you.

Dear Human,

Okay, you've read this book and thought, Oh, wow! Feel Good Club is right. I need some boundaries. I'm going to start putting them in place and I'm not going to feel guilty about it.

Great! Let's go.

And then somebody reacts to the boundaries you've put in place and you end up feeling guilty anyway.

So, here's the thing. When you've gone for so long without boundaries and you've allowed people to either take advantage of you or treat you in a way that you're not comfortable with, then they are going to be shocked when you start to say 'No', or make them aware that you no longer want to be treated that way.

It may take people a while to adjust, especially if you've lacked boundaries with them for a long time, but that's okay. We're not saying you need to break up with them or *unfriend* them straight away. They need time to learn your boundaries.

However, if they continue to disrespect your boundaries or react to your boundaries in a way that makes you feel guilty for having them, then it says far more about them than about you, and you definitely do not have to feel guilty about that.

You don't have to feel guilty for needing or asking for space.

FEEL GOOD TIP

Be patient with yourself once you start to set and action your boundaries, it doesn't happen overnight.

YOU DON'T HAVE TO FEEL GUILTY FOR NEEDING OR ASKING FOR SPACE.

Dear Human,

You need your own space. We all do.
It doesn't mean we don't love our partners,
that we want to leave our housemate and
never speak to them again, or that we hate
our best friends.

Admittedly, some of us need more space than others; as she's got older, Kiera has realised that she really loves her own space. For a long time, she felt guilty about it, and thought it meant she was antisocial, or boring, or that Aimie would think she didn't want to be around her.

Was any of that true? No. And is it better for a person's mental health to have time alone to process how they actually feel, rather than constantly surrounding themselves with others out of fear of upsetting them for needing me-time? Yes, far better actually.

And since Kiera has started making time for herself, does she feel better? Yes. She feels that certain things, along with others, like giving up alcohol and making healthier choices, is making her reconnect with herself and learn more about what she enjoys.

SOME OF US NEED MORE SPACE THAN OTHERS.

One of our best friends and colleagues, Jess, is our idol when it comes to alone time. Her one non-negotiable demand for moving in with her partner (who we also love) is that she had to have her own room – not like a 'Let's sleep in separate beds' scenario, just a spare room that she can go to when she feels like she needs to spend time alone, a night away, or a couple of hours reading a book, or doing something else she enjoys.

Does she feel guilty about it? No, because she knows that's what she needs and ultimately, that's going to make her relationship with herself and others better.

Communication is the key to everything, and as long as you communicate your needs in a way that allows your partners and friends to understand, then they should respect your wishes and you don't need to feel guilty.

TAKEAWAYS

1 Guilt is a normal human emotion.

2 Get into the habit of questioning why you feel guilty.

3 Do you feel guilty for something you've done wrong, or because you feel you *should* feel guilty?

9

Recognising what's important

Dear Human,

We spend a lot of time focusing on what's important to us. That's great. We need to do that. It makes us grow, thrive, want more, and maintain a life that we enjoy. But sometimes we have a blurred line between what's important and what isn't and we can end up fixating on things that really aren't important at all, taking up the energy and headspace we need to focus on what is.

You want to be liked. We get it. We do too. The thought of walking away from a situation and somebody saying bad things or feeling negatively about us makes us want to curl up and cry. But is it really that important?

WHAT PEOPLE SAY ABOUT YOU WHEN YOU'RE NOT AROUND SAYS MORE ABOUT THEM THAN YOU.

It's never nice to feel like somebody has something negative to say about you, but is it really important enough for you to spend the next day and a half thinking about it, when you actually don't even know if they said anything bad in the first place?

And does it really matter what they said anyway?

If you find yourself walking away from situations with people you trust and love, wondering whether they said anything bad about you, then maybe it's time to rethink that relationship.

Dear Human,

Numbers on your screen mean
absolutely nothing.

Likes and followers have zero impact on how good a person you are. They don't mean you're a better (or worse) person, but they've become a kind of currency, a measure for how popular or how beautiful we are – or think we are.

The only time we took followers into account was with the 'Travelling Story' we spoke about in an earlier chapter, when we made a deal with each other that if we didn't have 10,000 Instagram followers by the end of the year, we'd pack up and leave!

Just because we have a large following now doesn't make our business any better. It doesn't make our content any more helpful or knowledgeable, and it definitely doesn't mean we are more successful.

Stop comparing pixels on your screen to somebody else's. Whether that photo got one or 1,000 likes doesn't make it any more or less beautiful.

FEEL GOOD TIP

Social media platforms are used by so many of us, but try to make sure that this is a positive experience which adds something beneficial to your life. Have a monthly clearout of your following list and unfollow or mute accounts and content that have a negative impact on your day.

LIKES AND FOLLOWERS HAVE ZERO IMPACT ON HOW GOOD A PERSON YOU ARE.

Dear Human,

A friendship isn't a friendship, and a relationship isn't a relationship if you have to change yourself to be in it.

If you feel like you have to be someone else to fit in with your friendship group, then it's probably not made up of the important, lifelong bonds you think it is.

Our friendship group should be our safe space, the place where we can truly be ourselves. It should uplift us. At times, it might challenge us. Not all friendships will be smooth, but they are the relationships we usually hold to be the most important and that's a beautiful thing. However, we should also be aware that, for our own happiness and our own mental health, we need to know when these relationships no longer need to be regarded with the same importance they once were.

Because if people can't accept and love us for who we are, then they can't be that important in the first place.

FRIENDSHIP GROUPS SHOULD BE OUR SAFE SPACE, THE PLACE WHERE WE CAN TRULY BE OURSELVES.

Dear Human,

Your scales aren't important – unless medically required, of course.

We can't even remember the last time we weighed ourselves. As a result, we feel much more comfortable in our own skin and in our bodies and enjoy not having how we feel about ourselves be dictated by a unit of weight.

Our bodies change and fluctuate daily, weekly, monthly, and we're always aware when they do, so why place pressure on ourselves because of that?

If we had access to Room 101, weighing scales would go in there. They aren't important. You don't need them to love your body. Get rid of them.

Dear Human,

Burnout will get you nowhere.
Any workplace or client that expects
that of you in order to succeed doesn't
deserve your time or energy.

We have got to stop this toxic idea that to grow and prove ourselves we need to work ourselves to the bone.

It's very easy when you're running your own business, or doing a job that you love and you're passionate about, to want to go home and work after hours, especially when it's a project you're excited about. But if you're doing this, you need to form a clear boundary within yourself. Doing this when you're excited or passionate about a project is normal, but when it becomes something you do all the time, then setting an expectation for yourself that you will always be available is unhealthy and can lead to burnout.

The company isn't going to fall apart if you don't reply to that email and, if that were the case, I'm pretty sure someone would call you to ask for help anyway!

YOUR BOSS CAN WAIT. THE WORLD (OR THE COMPANY) IS NOT GOING TO FALL APART IF YOU DON'T REPLY.

TAKEAWAYS

1 Focus on caring less about what people think about you and more about what you think about yourself.

2 Get rid of your scales – or at least take the batteries out!

3 Set yourself a cut-off time for work and don't feel pressured to say 'Yes' to anything outside of that time . . . unless you really want to.

10

Feeling good, day by day, bit by bit

Dear Human,

Can you believe it? Here we are on the final chapter of this book!

Firstly, we want to say a massive thank you for making it this far, for supporting us, for soaking up our words, and for letting us be part of your journey. Secondly, we want to refer back to what we said somewhere near the beginning – that we didn't write this book as a tool to change anybody's life, because we don't have the skills, and it's not our place to tell you how to do that. We simply wrote it to let you know that what you feel in your darkest and happiest moments is completely normal, and to remind you that you're not alone.

We can only hope that we have done just that and that you will either keep this book somewhere close to you – in your bag, next to your bed, to pick up when you're feeling low – or that you'll pass it on to a friend, a stranger, anybody who might need it.

If you are working towards introducing positive changes into your life, be patient. Nothing happens overnight, so be kind to yourself. Growth is a process.

Change doesn't happen overnight and is worth being patient for. Let's consider New Year resolutions, such as 'New Year; new me' as an example. We spend 31 December each year deciding we're going to be a whole new person, but then we wake up on 1 January with the realisation that nothing has changed at all, and spend the next couple of weeks beating ourselves up that we aren't the person we said we were going to be.

Whether it's a new year, month, week, or day, you don't need to be a whole new person. You don't need to change yourself. Growth is about making small positive changes bit by bit, and this certainly doesn't happen overnight.

Positive change requires patience, bucketloads of it. The pressures of life take over. We have work to do, food to buy, meals to make, and it's easy to slip back into old routines and habits. You shouldn't beat yourself up about that.

FEEL GOOD TIP

Keep a Growth Diary, physical or mental, and keep track of how far you've come and of the things you've managed to change for the long term. When you notice yourself slipping, be kind to yourself, take a deep breath, acknowledge it, and try again.

Dear Human,

Life won't always go to plan –
it's not supposed to.

Don't expect to close this book and for your life to change immediately. You'll make mistakes. You'll forget to text back. Your heart will get broken. And some days you will feel as if nothing will ever be the same again.

But it will. Things will get better and you'll be strong enough to get through your darkest days.

You've probably noticed that throughout this book the word 'human' appears frequently, and that's what we want you to take away from this book – that everything you feel, every thought you have, the good and the bad ones, are all normal because you're a *human* being. And that's something we all have in common.

Humans forget to text back. We make mistakes. We say really dumb stuff. We get our hearts broken. We break the hearts of other people.

Things will get better and you'll be strong enough to get through your darkest days.

None of us have a handbook on how to be 'us', how to be human, how to deal with our mental health, how to become an adult and manage a zillion things at once.

And because there is no handbook, many of us haven't been told that it's okay if we make mistakes. It's okay that we don't quite know (or have any idea at all) what we're doing.

We're all figuring it out, bit by bit, day by day.

From two humans to another: Remember that you're not alone.

Dear Human,

*This is your life, your one and only life.
Every single thing about it is unique to you
and that is a beautifully exciting realisation.*

A bad day doesn't erase your progress. Bad days are normal. You will be okay. Self-care is knowing that 'your best' changes on a daily basis.

This is your life, your journey, your path. Don't miss the best bits by wishing it was somebody else's.

You want to change the world? I believe you can. You want to decide to have breakfast food for dinner? That's equally as exciting, because this is *your* life and nobody should have the power to tell you that you can't do anything you put your mind to.

Last week when out walking Juno, our dog, a jogger ran past us and looked like they were smashing it. Kiera's first thought was, *I wish I could run like them* – which, to be honest, was absolute bullsh*t because she hates running.

THIS IS YOUR LIFE, YOUR JOURNEY, YOUR PATH.

DON'T MISS THE BEST BITS BY WISHING IT WAS SOMEBODY ELSE'S.

Then we realised that we hardly ever see a runner actually stop – and if we do, it's a rare sighting. We never see them take a break, because then we just assume they are *walking* and *not* running.

We constantly see people at their best, in their flow. We see them *running*. We never see the break. We never see the sit down, the trying to catch breath.

The real success part is the ability to stop, the ability to realise when you need to come up for air and allow yourself a break. You don't get one without the other. You can't do it all without a break.

FINAL TAKEAWAYS

As we end this book, we want to leave you with these thoughts:

- Every journey, every life, has peaks and troughs.

- And every journey, every life, is special, unique and absolutely beautiful.

- We should all have the ability to live our life in the way we want to.

- And although we don't all have the same opportunities and head starts, we are all human and have the ability to accept and love ourselves, and each other, for just that – being human.

All our love,
    Aimie and Kiera

Acknowledgements

Our Families

Howard Lord

Atul Bansal

Jessica Mannion

Tash Mills

Our whole Feel Good team

Juno Lawlor-Skillen

Hannah Anderson

Steven Bartlett

Doddz

Beth Trundle

Katy Leeson

Aino Raittinen

Paul Shakeshaft

Hattie Pearson

Sam McGowan

Christie Childers

Adam Parsons

Stephen Pankhurst

Sidari Reddy

Shadene Hutchinson

Suman Matharu

Charlotte Hunt

Sarah O'Connor

Kylie and Kris

Murph and Jordan

Stephanie Pryce

Sheep

Victoria Shaw

Icon Embroidery

Heart and Graft

Richy Edwards

Jamie Butler

Lorna Saxon

Claudia Mirallegro

Joe Flinders

Dom Mcgregor

Clare Bethan

ACKNOWLEDGEMENTS

Our neighbours – thanks for putting
our bins out when we didn't have time.

To our beautiful supporters and regulars,
who keep us going and brighten every single day.

The team at HarperCollins – Ola Galewicz,
Eve Hutchings, Megan Donaghy, Gale Winskill
and Essie Cousins.

Bengono Bessala – thank you for bringing
our dream to reality.

Ways to improve your day:

1

Drink water.

2

Steer clear of negative
conversation.

3

Only say yes if you mean it.

4

Don't rush.

5

Commit to being your
complete + whole self without
changing for anyone else
around you.

YOUR ENERGY IS PHENOMENAL.

A lack of motivation today doesn't make you a lazy person, a bad day today doesn't mean you're not happy. Everything fluctuates. Be kind to yourself.

THE WORLD IS A BETTER PLACE WITH YOU IN IT.

Notes

....
....
....
....
....
....
....
....
....
....
....
....
....

Notes

....
....
....
....
....
....
....
....
....
....
....
....
....
....

Notes

....

....

....

....

....

....

....

....

....

....

....

....

....

Notes

....

....

....

....

....

....

....

....

....

....

....

....

....

....

Notes

....

....

....

....

....

....

....

....

....

....

....

....

....

....

Notes

....

....

....

....

....

....

....

....

....

....

....

....

....